WOMEN WHO CHANGED THE WORLD

The Journey and the Joy

CRANBROOK SCHOOLS

SUNBURY PRESS

Mechanicsburg, PA USA

Published by Sunbury Press, Inc.
50 West Main Street
Mechanicsburg, Pennsylvania 17055

SUNBURY PRESS

www.sunburypress.com

For information about special discounts for bulk purchases, please contact Sunbury Press Orders Dept. at (855) 338-8359 or orders@sunburypress.com.

To request one of our authors for speaking engagements or book signings, please contact Sunbury Press Publicity Dept. at publicity@sunburypress.com.

ISBN: 978-1-62006-597-6 (Hard cover)

FIRST SUNBURY PRESS EDITION: May 2015

Product of the United States of America
0 1 1 2 3 5 8 13 21 34 55

Set in Bookman Old Style
Designed by Crystal Devine
Cover by Lawrence Knorr
Edited by Janice Rhayem

Continue the Enlightenment!

CONTENTS

FOREWORD

This book started as the "Cranbrook project" led by one of the parents, Gerard Mantese. The Cranbrook project was created through the efforts of a group of determined Cranbrook eighth-grade girls. Our journey began by our wondering how some women have achieved greatness, and what we can do to make our own mark on the world. We decided to examine this question and contacted women who have achieved great things. We talked with many extraordinary women. They inspired us with their focus, energy, and creativity. They explained that, sometimes, your life may take a different turn, but you should fearlessly embrace a new road to achieve your goals. We are pleased to share our experience with others through the publication of this book. We hope you enjoy this glimpse into the lives of the women who generously gave of their time and graciously shared their adventures and inspirations. What we have learned will follow us forever: Defeat is never an option; Passion for your work is critical; Giving back to others is necessary.

The Authors
June 2015

ACKNOWLEDGMENTS

The authors would like to extend their gratitude to many individuals for their helpful guidance and overall enthusiasm for this project. We wish to acknowledge our sincerest thanks to the great and dynamic women who unselfishly gave of their time to talk to us and give us their insights about the world around us. We also thank Sarah Hulett, assistant news director at Michigan Radio, for her discussion with the authors about interviewing techniques. We also thank Lauren Messner, our photographer, for some of the photographs, for her artistry, and patience. We also appreciate Brenda Ren for her many hours in coordinating schedules, handling administrative matters, and working with us to put this book together.

We want to give our special thanks to Stacy Rivard, head of the Girls Middle School, and Nola-Rae Cronan, dean of the Girls Middle School, Cranbrook Schools, for their advice, insights, and enthusiastic support for this project. We realize that we are truly blessed to be part of the Cranbrook community.

Finally, to the Cranbrook parents, we appreciate the many ways they supported us throughout this process and for holding a secure and loving place in the authors' hearts.

DR. SUE CARTER

"If you follow your passion, then what you do really isn't work," Dr. Sue Carter explains. Do what you love, and you will enjoy your job. For Dr. Carter, she has followed the passion of public service. She quotes the age-old words of Mahatma Gandhi: "The best way to find yourself, is to lose yourself in the service of others." Throughout her life, Dr. Sue Carter has taken every opportunity to serve, following the wind to the next opportunity, creating chances to improve the world. This is the essence of Dr. Carter.

Dr. Carter recalls as a child being motivated by her mother's words, "The water buffalo are waiting at the gate. Let's go!" These words were intended to provide her with a mainspring to seize life's experiences. She reflects that her mother was a great source of inspiration for her, and her wisdom guided her through the years. As a child, Dr. Carter had the opportunity to live in France when she was seven years of age. This experience was the start of her lifelong love of travel and of knowledge about a variety of cultures and places throughout the world.

Dr. Carter embraces education, having been awarded a bachelor's degree in humanities and then her master's degree in humanities from Michigan State University. She also received her juris doctorate degree from Wayne State University, was ordained a priest in the Episcopal Church, and received a doctor of ministry degree from Seabury Western Theological Seminary.

Her cultivated education has given Dr. Carter the opportunity to be a leader in many diverse environments. Her accomplishments include appointment to secretary of the Board of Trustees, executive assistant to

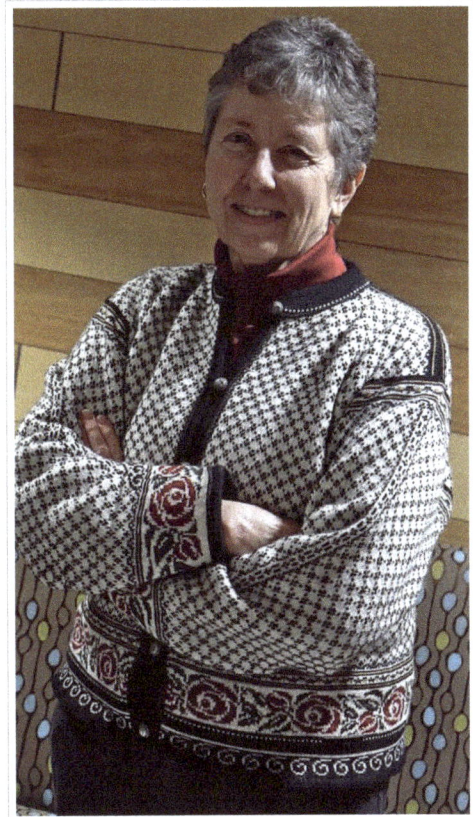

Michigan State presidents Peter McPherson and Lou Anna Simon, and appointment to press secretary to Michigan Governor James Blanchard.

Her organizational skills are unprecedented and include the spearheading of the first all women ski expedition from Russia to the North Pole. When asked why she pursued this venture, she responded, "There's something about being the first. We're smart girls, we don't need a man." This North Pole expedition gained worldwide momentum, generating excitement for gender equality about science, technology, engineering, and math. She and her team of twelve other women went on the breathtaking venture in which they reported back to classrooms via satellite phone throughout their journey and finally via a webcast assisted by NASA when they reached the North Pole. Another global venture that Dr. Carter led was the production of the Emmy winning *Malaria in Malawi: Fighting to Save the Children.* This is a documentary of childhood malaria in Malawi and the work of Michigan State University's Dr. Terrie Taylor in treating and studying the disease in Malawi.

Dr. Carter is currently a professor at the School of Journalism at Michigan State University where she also serves as the faculty athletic representative to the National College Athletic Association. Dr. Carter takes pride in her teaching. She explains, "I've been teaching going on 25 years now ... I like to teach: sharing ideas with others and seeing where they take those ideas. Those things inspire me, to see others be able to fulfill their potential."

With all these accomplishments, the leadership role that gives Dr. Carter the most pride is the leadership she has learned from belonging to a family. Quoting Robert Frost, she said, "Family is where they have to take you in." She frequently reflects warmly and proudly on her daughter and grandchildren whom she deeply cherishes. As a child, Dr. Carter learned the importance of helping others. In raising her daughter, she attempted to exemplify the importance of service: she recalls that when her daughter was younger, she and her daughter worked in a soup kitchen together as well as other mission projects. She hopes to inspire the same desire in her grandchildren to serve someday. From being a mother, to a professor, to a journalist, to an explorer, whatever Dr. Sue Carter embarks on, she seems to find the magic in that experience to be able to serve and to change the world for good. This is what makes her a truly exceptional woman.

When asked what advice she would give to women in leadership roles, Dr. Carter gave two pieces of essential advice. She explained that women have a unique ability to collaborate. "Our lives are fluid, we share our experiences, I think, better than men do. So, build on that talent, that ability." Her second piece of advice was to make lists. She advises making a list every night before going to bed outlining the next day. "It can be fun stuff," she adds. The idea is that these lists keep the writer focused,

knowing exactly what they seek to accomplish the next day. "So make a list before you go to bed tonight. What does tomorrow look like?"

Sue Carter has seen the world. She has traveled throughout it, yet she can still say the world is getting better. "It's not to say we don't have wars and conflicts, we still have famine, but a lot more people have clean water to drink than when I was a child. The threat of nuclear war, I think, is pretty much in the past; it certainly is not current. I saw a lot of people reaching out, you know, when there was the earthquake in Haiti. Some people get it wrong, but a lot of people do some staggeringly important things." This focus, the ability to see that positive things are happening for our world, is essential. Not only does Dr. Carter see the change, she makes herself part of it. She throws herself into public service, creates opportunities, and makes and strengthens ties. This is a key part of her, and the lesson we all can take from her. See the change for the better, recognize it, and encourage it with your own actions.

"If you follow your passion, then what you do really isn't work."

—Dr. Sue Carter

MAMATHA CHAMARTHI

Mamatha Chamarthi is a successful technology executive living in Michigan. Originally from the State of Andhra Pradesh in India, her natural talent in sales, marketing, and business thinking landed her an executive position in April of 2014 as vice president and chief information officer, or CIO, of TRW Automotive Holdings Corporation. TRW is a diversified supplier of automotive systems, modules, and components to global automotive original equipment manufacturers, or OEMs. The Livonia, Michigan-based company employs 60,000 people in approximately 190 major facilities around the world, and is ranked among the top ten automotive suppliers in the world.

Chamarthi has been an influential member of the IT community for the past two decades. While at a former position at Daimler Financial Services, she transformed the company's supply chain management processes, resulting in $28.4 million of annual cost savings, which eventually culminated in her being featured in several IT magazines. She began her career as a programmer and analyst, moving up through the ranks by demonstrating clear leadership skills and tackling difficult technological challenges.

Prior to TRW, Chamarthi was appointed VP and CIO of CMS Energy and its principal subsidiary, Consumers Energy, in May 2010, taking over responsibility for the company's information technology systems. She also spends a lot of time helping to advance women in technology through mentoring and speaking engagements. She spent three years as a VP of Strategy and Operations of the Michigan Council of Women in Technology, a nonprofit devoted to advancing women's interests in the business community, and helped launch the nonprofit's summer mentorship program. She has a wide range of educational qualifications including a master's degree in English literature, computer science, and an MBA from

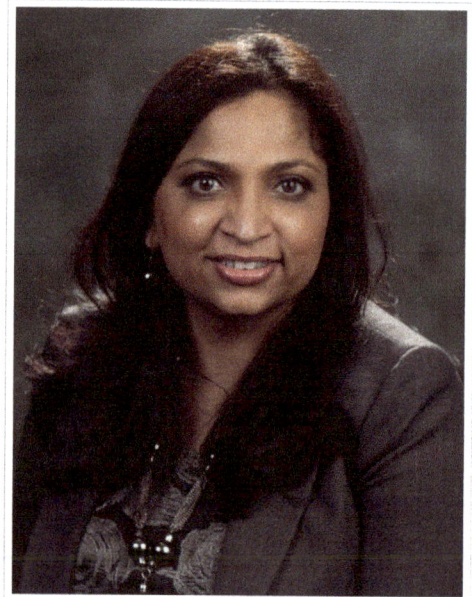

prestigious institutes both in India and the United States.

When asked, "What motivated you to become a CIO," Chamarthi said, "My mentor, Mrs. Unger from Chrysler who gave me the inspiration." Chamarthi added that she has learned many things from Mrs. Unger during her Chrysler days. Her natural talent of looking at any problem from a "business" perspective allowed her to succeed in delivering anything given to her, and other executives immediately recognized the traits of an executive in her. She even remembers her programming days when her boss gave her a small programming project; she kept asking several piercing questions relating to the business and benefits of writing the program—the answers shook her boss's thought process.

When asked, "How do you make people who work for you listen to you?" Chamarthi, without any hesitation, said, "Knowledge." If you are more knowledgeable, people will listen to you. She advised everyone to gain knowledge by reading a lot. To reiterate this point, she jokingly stated that some people need to be spoon fed certain technical concepts. She said that she is an avid reader and keeps reading several books even today. In fact, she even has eBooks on her smartphone and reads them whenever she gets an opportunity. She recommended the book *On Becoming Fearless … in Love, Work, and Life* by Arianna Huffington.

Chamarthi encourages girls to strongly consider a career in STEM (an acronym for science, technology, engineering, and mathematics). When asked, "What advice can you give for middle school girls for a career," she started explaining her experiences with driving a semi-automated truck in a testing ground with her iPad by sitting in the passenger seat with no driver! She sees a lot of future for engineering careers, and plans to build several products for TRW and continue to grow the company. In support of her mission to help young women, she extended an open invitation to the middle school girls for a tour of TRW whenever they are interested. When asked, "What are your top challenges or goals in the current CIO position," she replied that her immediate challenges are closing current acquisitions and focusing on the company's products to help make the company profitable.

And when asked, "How do you manage the work-life balance while holding such a responsible executive position," she replied, "By division of labor," and proudly says that she loves and enjoys cooking for the family while the other family members—her husband and her two children—take care of other household chores.

"Don't be afraid to take chances and do not say no to an opportunity."

—Mamatha Chamarthi

JUSTICE MAURA CORRIGAN

"Do what needs to be done. <u>There is no they, only we.</u> WE have the power to fix things," said Justice Maura Corrigan. She is the perfect example of this statement. Justice Corrigan served two terms as a Michigan Supreme Court justice, including a term as chief justice. She later served as the head of the Michigan Department of Human Services (DHS.) In these roles, Justice Corrigan made a significant impact on the state of Michigan, especially with respect to the care of foster children. As a judge, she thoughtfully managed more than 30,000 cases. During the time she was the head of the DHS, the department had over two million clients and employed twelve thousand people! Receiving three hundred to four hundred e-mails a day, it was a very demanding job. During her tenure, critical changes were made, including reduction of the welfare budget from $7 billion to $5.6 billion (a savings of $1.4 billion for the state.)

Justice Corrigan was the eldest of seven daughters. Her mother was a nurse, and her father was a physician and teacher at a medical school in Ohio. During her early childhood, her favorite pastime was to read. She would save up the money she earned from her chores to buy Nancy Drew books. She loved reading Nancy Drew and dreamed of one day becoming a detective. In the summers, Justice Corrigan worked at her dad's office, where she enjoyed helping people. During high school, she decided that she wanted to become a doctor, and she shared this aspiration with her father. It was not traditional for a woman to be a physician, but Justice Corrigan loved medicine. Her father refused to send her to medical school, because he said that it would "take a man's seat," and he refused to support her. This was a heartbreaking experience, but it prepared her for additional challenges later

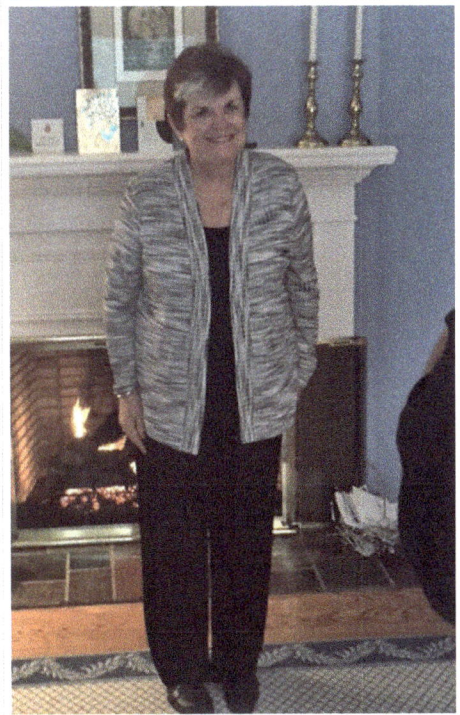

in life. After much thought, she decided to go to law school, and her love for both medicine and law helped her accomplish her goals.

When we asked about her sources of motivation, she said that her mother is her main source of support and that she taught her to be brave. She gave an example of her mother's courage one day when they were having lunch together and a robbery occurred in the bank building next door to them. While everyone else was fleeing for their lives, her mother was administering first aid to a person who had been injured onsite at the robbery. This example of her mother's courage was one of the greatest inspirations in her life. She believes that Governor John Engler's quote summarizes this principle: "Your life expands in proportion to your courage."

Justice Corrigan encourages everyone to think positively, stating, "Try to find the good things in tragedy." Thirteen years ago, Judge Corrigan lost her husband to a relentless and ongoing disease. She spoke of tender and heartfelt moments with her husband before he died. She shared a poignant sentiment: "I would never trade anything for my marriage to my wonderful husband. Nothing at all." Now looking back, Justice Corrigan believes that this tragedy has bonded the family and taught her to cherish each day.

Justice Maura Corrigan's faith is a big part of her daily life. She believes that we owe compassion to each other and that our purpose is to serve and to love. One of Justice Corrigan's favorite authors is C. S. Lewis. C. S. Lewis once said that "God is Love and we are all reflections of God's love." Justice Corrigan believes that every child deserves to grow up in a loving home. This made her an excellent choice to become the head of DHS, because it involved the foster care system and children who really needed a caring individual to guide their well-being.

She and DHS made great strides in many ways. By the time she left the department, 90 percent of the children in the system were being adopted. She and her team worked to lower the suicide rate for children as well. Twelve years ago the majority of children in the system dropped out of high school, but by the end of her tenure, she reversed this trend with the vast majority of children successfully graduating from high school. Justice Corrigan and the DHS formed partnerships with local colleges to enable foster care children to pursue a college education. She understood the needs and special situations of foster children and she worked relentlessly to make a positive impact in their lives.

One of the many things Justice Corrigan teaches everyone is to always have faith in yourself. No matter what happens, she stated, "Always have faith that you will do well and you will succeed." She also said that appearance will not always help you, but your virtues will. This is important to young girls today, because many feel that they need to "plaster on the makeup and curl their hair more times than needed" in order to be successful and popular. Justice Corrigan believes that if you have good intentions and are willing to help, people will trust and befriend you.

She described the importance of friendships in her life and how those partnerships fostered ideas and new opportunities. Her favorite quote by William Butler Yeats relates to this: "Think where man's glory most begins and ends, and say my glory was I had such friends." This quote tells us that true friendships are the most glorious gifts of all. She advocates that individuals should always be brave and courageous. She said, "Be everything you can be! Go for it! And most importantly, believe in yourself! Settle for more, don't settle for less." She emphasized how important it is to never falter or give up on your dreams … no matter what stands in your way.

Justice Corrigan has recently been selected to be involved in a Washington DC "think tank" called The American Enterprise Institute, which is managed by Paul Ryan, who is the chairman of the House Way and Means Committee. Their main goal is to identify ways to help the poor transform their lives for the better. Justice Corrigan states that "the war on poverty" is still happening … and poverty is winning. Over $20 trillion has been spent to help the poor. Yet, these funds have made virtually no impact on the lives of the poor. She, along with many others, hope to find a way to help the impoverished, not with just food stamps or welfare, but to permanently transform their lives.

Justice Corrigan hopes to leave a legacy to guide strong, young women who will take charge and never let anyone get in their way. "Who do you want to be? Who do you want to become? These are the questions you need to ask yourself when you are in a rough patch." Justice Maura Corrigan is an inspiration for everyone. She is a person who has changed our world.

"Do what needs to be done. There is no they, only we. We have the power to fix things."

—Justice Maura Corrigan

MILDRED DRESSELHAUS

Dr. Mildred Dresselhaus is an acclaimed scientist and female leader. She states, "I wake up each morning with a smile on my face because this is what I want to do." Dr. Dresselhaus has carefully carved out a career that is still heavily dominated by men. It is hard to imagine how a young girl could come to be one of the most sought-after physicists of this generation. She has made amazing breakthroughs throughout her life and continues to inspire women even today. Dr. Dresselhaus believes that her career path is not going to be unique in the future. She is optimistic that more women will make their mark in science and on the world stage.

Dr. Dresselhaus said that she was always encouraged to pursue her love of science, even though this field is predominantly male. When asked why she decided to pursue a career in physics, she said that it was purely interest and joy. She strove to understand this seemingly complicated scientific field, because she found it exciting, and she felt compelled to understand the world in the context of scientific principles. For Dr. Dresselhaus, this scientific exploration is not work—it is fun. In her early research days, she describes how working in the laboratory gave her hours and years of pleasure.

When Mildred was a small girl, she lived in New York, in a suburb of the city. She was not rich, and her parents were not educated. She went to school with all of the other poor children, and her situation was quite common. The only thing to distinguish her from all of the other children in her neighborhood was her violin and a scholarship to music school. At seven years old, Mildred found music school a hardship, along with the commute in New York City through four public transit interchanges. She faced these challenges at seven years old.

Mildred was able to meet children who had the resources to enroll in the better New York programs. These new friends helped her to research and to prepare for the entrance exams that would open the door to stronger schools and a brighter future. Suddenly, Mildred went from the worst schools in New York to the very best schools. Even still, with limited opportunities for even the brightest women, her dream was to be a schoolteacher. This goal came easy to Mildred as she took a job as a tutor to other students to supplement her family's income.

Academically, she was an excellent student and received high grades. She recalled that she was better at math, but continued in science, because she liked science better than math. Her joy in learning math and science did not mean that these subjects did not require her to study hard to understand the principles of these disciplines. During most of the eleventh grade, she was quarantined because of whooping cough, a disease which is now preventable. She missed many classes during that time and had a hard year, consequently. Another factor that made it hard was that she was the only girl in her class at Harvard College. Officially, she attended Radcliffe College, a sister school to Harvard, as girls were not allowed admission at Harvard. Yet, she was able to take Harvard classes as a Radcliffe student. Many of her classes had only boys, who were not always welcoming, so this was a challenge. Despite the challenges, however, she was able to progress in her studies.

Dr. Dresselhaus was a part of a significant experiment that proved the importance of carbon nanotubes. She showed how the nanotubes conduct heat and electricity more efficiently than regular carbon. Because of her discovery, scientists now know how to define and characterize graphite, graphene, and carbon nanotubes. She was given many awards for her work and is now retired. Yet, even though having retirement status, she continues to work at Massachusetts Institute of Technology. Every morning she attends work to connect with her students. She conducts seminars, holds appointments, and helps teachers and students. She believes that it is important to "teach the students to become teachers."

MILDRED SPIEWAK
Any equation she can solve;
Every problem she can resolve.
Mildred equals brains plus fun,
In math and science she's second to
none.

When asked what advice she would give young women, Mildred responded, "Keep doing what you're interested in, whatever it is. Staying busy [keeps you healthy]." Dr. Dresselhaus believes anyone can do anything with a strong mindset and a heart full of determination. "Women who change the world? We all are." And she is absolutely correct. We all are women who have changed, and can and will, change the world.

Dr. Dresselhaus's name draws inspiration to scientists around the world. Her work has helped shape further carbon nanotube experiments. Even today, she helps students pursue their own scientific careers. Dr. Dresselhaus is an exemplary character in science today. Everything she has done has advanced future discoveries and technology. She believes working hard will pay off. She did work very hard, and she has made significant contributions in science that will help us all.

"I wake up each morning with a smile on my face because this is what I want to do."

—Mildred Dresselhaus

KATHARINE HAYHOE

Dr. Katharine Hayhoe is an exceptional scientist whose work is focused on atmospheric climate change. Dr. Hayhoe is the chief executive officer and founder of ATMOS Research. She has also served as scientific advisor for the Energy and Enterprise Initiative, the Evangelical Eco to Citizen's Climate Lobby America Environmental Network, and the International Women's Earth and Climate Initiative: *The Momentous*.

Her work bridges the gap between scientists and stakeholders. She and her husband, Andrew Farley, wrote, *A Climate for Change: Global Warming Facts for Faith Based Decisions*. This book was intended to help answer the complex questions that have emerged as to the interrelationship between climate change and faith. Dr. Hayhoe believes that science and faith are like two sides of a coin, "Science is the evidence of everything that we can see, quantify, and measure. Science is everything that we can observe. Faith is by definition intangible, everything that we cannot see, observe, or measure. So they are not competing with each other because they are doing completely different things." Dr. Hayhoe has published over one hundred papers and has been featured in two documentaries: *Living Dangerously* and *The Secret Life of Scientists*. She has been named as one of the "Time 100: The Most Influential 100 People" for 2014, and currently works for the Texas Tech University as the director of the Climate Change Center.

Dr. Hayhoe grew up in Canada. As a child, she did not have her own television. Every weekend her mother would go to the local library and borrow old films. Her favorites were the Jane Goodall movies. She marveled over Goodall's inspiring work with her chimpanzees, and that a young woman could live alone in Africa practicing good science and doing what she loved. Katharine Hayhoe said her favorite quote is from Jane Goodall, "Only when our clever brain and our human heart work together in harmony do we achieve our full potential."

When she was ten, she moved to Columbia. There she grew to appreciate the impact of weather when spending so much time outdoors. She met a wide variety of people and made many friends. Some of her friends were very well off and even had cars or cellphones. Others were not as well off and lived in huts made of mud or straw. Some even lived in shacks made of cardboard boxes. When there was a flood, their little hut would collapse. Dr. Hayhoe learned that the climate can drastically change people's lives. She came to realize how vulnerable many people in the world are to significant climate events. She decided she would make people understand that we are the ones who are causing climate change, and we need to act.

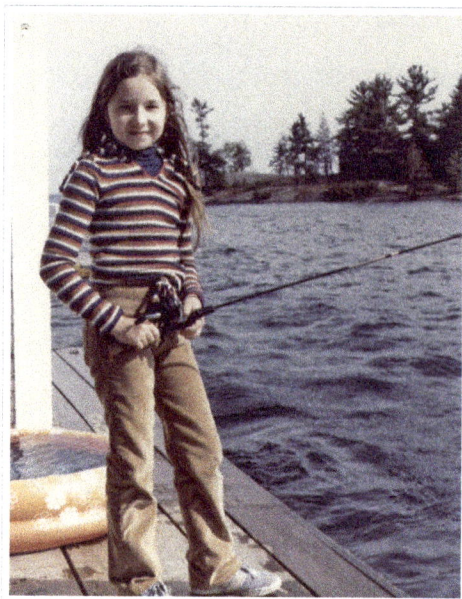

Dr. Hayhoe's unique combination of being a scientist and a Christian allows her to have a wonderful strategy for working with people who disagree with her views. She said that she talks to people every day who disagree with her views. She understands that there are reasons that they feel or believe the way that they do. She looks for the things that they can agree on first. By finding common ground, she then can start asking questions about why they believe what they do and then can begin to provide more information. "Often times I can honestly say that: 'yeah' if that was true I would not agree either, but let me tell you why it is not true," Katharine Hayhoe said.

About ten years ago, Katharine Hayhoe did a study for the state of California where she looked at specific ways in which climate change would impact the state, such as how climate would affect air quality, water, farmers, food production, and natural resources. The study showed a comparison of what would happen if there were no changes and the benefit of making changes to reduce carbon emissions. Because of the study, California's governor enacted laws and made concrete changes to reduce carbon emissions. Katharine Hayhoe is very proud of this study because of the measurable positive impact it has had on California.

Like many successful women, Katharine Hayhoe had much to say when it came to advice. "Don't always stick to the plan, because you only get to the better things when you don't." Dr. Hayhoe's plan was to become a physicist; however, she actually became an atmospheric scientist. In fact,

Dr. Hayhoe believes that her life is based on a series of accidents, and that her life is much better with these unplanned events. Dr. Hayhoe has taught us that we should always be open minded, because an open mind is crucial to success. She also attributes much of her success to her curiosity. She said, "Curiosity leads you to explore new things, try new things, learn new things, do new things."

Dr. Hayhoe is an inspiration for all people, especially women. Throughout her career, Dr. Hayhoe has helped the world in many ways with her groundbreaking work on climate change and her insightful views on religion and science. She is a gifted person, who is a role model for other young people, especially young girls. She said, "We cannot change the world all by ourselves as individuals, so we need to work together and we need to get good laws and policies in place to help us do the right things." Dr. Hayhoe's message is for all to hear and all to ponder as we face the critical questions on how climate has come to have effects on everyone's life.

"Don't always stick to the plan, because you only get to the better things when you don't."

—Katharine Hayhoe

FLORINE MARK

Ask Florine Mark, president and CEO of The WW Group, Inc., about her childhood and one word comes to mind: FatFlo. As a young girl growing up in a poor neighborhood of Detroit, Florine's life was vastly different from the life she leads today. Living in a crowded home with fourteen relatives, including her mother, father, grandparents, her six aunts and uncles, two sisters, and one disabled uncle, young Florine was known among the kids in the neighborhood for her weight, thus her nickname FatFlo.

As a teenager still struggling with her weight, Florine began to take diet pills quite regularly. In fact, she once took so many pills she was rushed to the hospital where the doctor told her, "I'm not in charge of your life ..." and that if she died the fault would be her own. Those words, she said, inspired her to think about how she could manage her weight loss in a healthy, responsible, structured way.

Her thoughts turned to what her grandmother, who was her role model, and other family members always told her: "Florine, you can do anything you want as long as you want it bad enough." But the expectations have to be reasonable. In fact, this is the motto that she uses to this day.

Married and raising five children, Florine was frustrated by her inability to lose weight when she heard about a weight loss group that began in New York City in 1963 called Weight Watchers where participants met regularly to discuss weight loss challenges and provide support for one another, as well as learn healthy dieting tips. Florine flew to New York in July 1966, where she attended fifteen classes in five days and then meetings once a month for four months during which time she lost forty pounds. That was

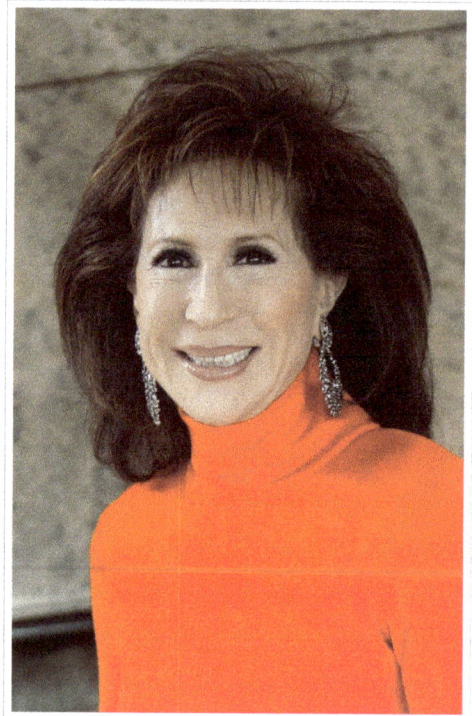

relatively easy compared to losing the last ten pounds of her goal; that took a year.

After losing the weight and gaining confidence, Jean Nidetch, founder of Weight Watchers, encouraged Florine to take the Weight Watchers concept to Detroit. Florine did just that, holding her first meeting in a school gymnasium. Now, almost fifty years later, that one meeting has grown into a company called WW Group, Inc., the largest franchiser of Weight Watchers International, holding meetings throughout Michigan and Ontario, Canada.

Knowing the struggles people face in trying to lose weight, Florine is most proud of the success stories she hears from members, many of which bring tears to her eyes. "It is the best feeling ever," she said.

Focusing on the good is a big part of Florine's life. "I don't dwell on the negative," she said, adding that this positive spirit motivates her charity work. Whenever she has a moment of free time, she tries her best to spend it doing charity work. She also hosts a radio talk show, *Remarkable Women*, which airs across Michigan, and communicates directly with Weight Watchers members via "Ask Florine" on Twitter.

Beyond time at the office and charity work, Florine takes time for herself. She enjoys exercising—especially walking—and traveling, as well as spending time with her family and grandchildren. She also spends time each morning "talking to the mirror." Being such a high profile, influential businesswoman, Florine is an expert at speaking in public, whether to a large group or small gatherings. She is known for her inspirational words and people who have known Florine for years, or who have just met her, are impressed by her candor, upbeat attitude, and belief that anything is possible. When she's not speaking to others, though, she maintains the ability to encourage others by encouraging herself ... after waking each morning, she looks at herself in her mirror and talks to herself about the day ahead, goals, anything to motivate her to succeed and help those around her do and be their best.

As a successful woman in the world of business, Florine is often asked by other professional women what they can do to succeed. She advises them to have a good attitude about themselves, to give of their time, to love others, and to have exceptional character. Her recommendations also include

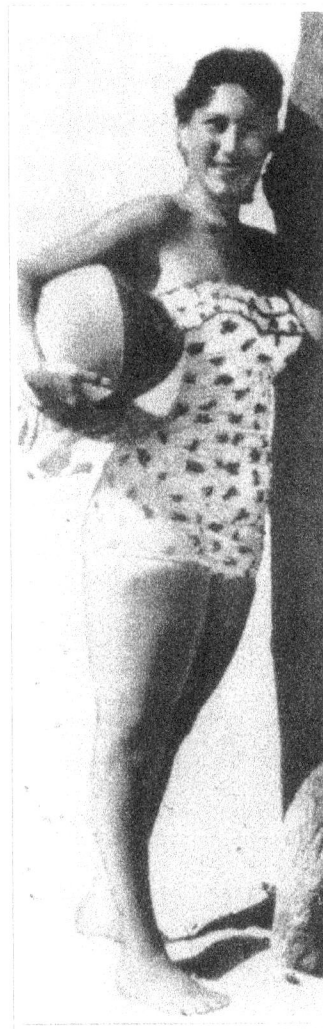

networking with other successful women and being flexible enough to modify goals and the paths to achieve them.

Florine Mark, from her corner of the world in Farmington Hills, Michigan, is motivated to change the world, change people's attitudes about weight and self-image, and, most important, change their thoughts about self-acceptance ... to love who they are each and every day on their journey to becoming the best version of themselves.

"I don't dwell on the negative."

—Florine Mark

JUSTICE BRIDGET MCCORMACK

Bridget Mary McCormack is a Justice of the Michigan Supreme Court. She has been a Justice since January 1, 2013. She has also received the prestigious 12th Annual Guardian of Justice Award. At forty-eight years of age, Justice McCormack has already achieved remarkable success, though she is modest about her achievements.

Bridget McCormack was born in Washington, DC and was raised in Plainfield, New Jersey. Her mother is a clinical social worker, and her father is a former United States Marine. She has two siblings, Mary, who is an accomplished actress, best known for her role on *The West Wing*, and Will, who is both an actor and screenwriter.

Bridget McCormack attended high school in central New Jersey and received a bachelor of arts with honors in political science and philosophy from Trinity College in Connecticut in 1988. She received her juris doctorate from New York University Law School, where she was a Root-Tilden Scholar and won the Anne Petluck Poses Prize in clinical advocacy. She spent the first five years of her legal career in New York, first as a trial counsel at the Legal Aid Society, and then at the Office of the Appellate Defender. From 1997 to 1998, Bridget McCormack taught at Yale Law School. In 1998 she became a professor at the University of Michigan Law School. While at the University of Michigan, she created several new clinics, including on domestic violence, pediatric advocacy, and other practical education development projects, while also becoming associate dean of the law school.

Justice McCormack is married to Steven Croley, a lawyer and a law professor at the University of Michigan Law School, who is currently on leave in Washington DC to serve as general counsel to the U.S. Department of Energy. Together, Steven and Bridget have four children: John, Anna, Matthew, and Harry.

In 2008 Bridget McCormack cofounded the Michigan Innocence Clinic. During her tenure with the organization, she received numerous awards. The Michigan Innocence Clinic investigates cases with new evidence that could prove the innocence of wrongly convicted prisoners. The organization focuses efforts on cases that involve non-DNA evidence. Justice McCormack is proud of the work that this group is conducting, although she is unable to personally continue to assist the organization, given her current role on the Michigan Supreme Court.

Justice McCormack spoke of a very special case involving David Lee Gavitt. He was a man who had been exonerated after spending twenty-seven years in prison for the wrongful conviction of setting a fire in his home, which resulted in the deaths of his wife and two young daughters. The experts testified that this was a case of arson, though no motive was ever proven. The Innocence Clinic was able to use new scientific evidence to demonstrate that this was not a gasoline-fueled fire, nor was there any evidence to suggest that a crime had been committed by Mr. Gavitt.

Perhaps most heartbreaking about this story was how Mr. Gavitt, upon release from prison just days after his fifty-fourth birthday, left the prison, free for the first time in twenty-seven years. His first action was to visit the graves of his wife and children. Though Justice McCormack no longer works with the clinic, she strongly believes in the work the clinic is doing, and is moved by the continued stories of justice being served.

In 2014 Justice McCormack was appointed by the U.S. Department of Justice and the U.S. Department of Commerce to a National Commission on Forensic Science. She was excited that she was asked to be one of the members of this ground-breaking organization. The group is comprised of both scientists and law-makers, working to develop policy recommendations for the U.S. attorney general. The commission works to improve the practice of forensic science. This seems a natural extension of the work Justice McCormack was doing at the Michigan Innocence Clinic, utilizing new technology, science, and research to define new regulatory processes and procedures.

Justice McCormack is a woman with integrity, work ethic, and energy. She is successful in dealing with all kinds of people. She cares deeply about justice, not just for some citizens, but for all. This profound belief in fairness was shaped at an early age and has guided her entire career. When asked, "What is the source of your inspiration?" Justice McCormack's immediate response was, "My parents." Her father, who was a marine and a small-business owner, worked extremely hard, seven days a week, for his entire life. Her mother was a social worker, who also was committed to her work and her family.

Even at an early age, Justice McCormack was taught the importance of community. When Bridget was a young girl in middle school, she came

home to find a stranger in the house. There was a woman who was obviously beaten and bruised, the victim of domestic abuse. She realized her mom had volunteered to take this woman in to live with them because it was not safe for her to go home. Justice McCormack said the experience opened her eyes to the importance of social justice and fairness. She appreciated that her mother was an individual possessing a strong commitment to giving back and improving the community. This inspirational act was Justice McCormack's major motivation to work pro bono and to build community.

Justice McCormack states, "I am passionate about my career and devoted to my family. Balance is something moms know innately. I don't want to give up any of my commitment to my work, and I don't want to give up any time parenting my kids for the brief period they are living with us." Justice McCormack explained that there are times when extra effort is required for work activities. This became obvious to her when she campaigned to be a Michigan Supreme Court justice. There are also other times when family must be the priority. For example, when her son was hospitalized for a lengthy period of time to evaluate the cause of his seizures, Justice McCormack had to be at her son's side.

When questioned about past mistakes, Justice McCormack was thoughtful in her response. Apart from an embarrassing haircut in high school, her feeling was that she has been fortunate throughout her life. She does not look at any of her work or life choices as mistakes, but rather learning experiences. Even in challenging situations, as when her child was hospitalized, she finds the positive. In those agonizing days observing her helpless child in a hospital bed, Justice McCormack was able to spend additional time with her son and be with him in his time of need. Her response to this question was inspirational.

Justice McCormack is passionate about her achievements. She taught us that there is no one path for women to follow in law—you must make your own path. She leads by example, advocating for families with sick children, victims of domestic violence, and ordinary people who are in need of help. She is a positive force in her service on Michigan's Supreme Court. It is her passion for her career that she hopes will influence her children and is motivated by the idea that you can make a difference, and you can love what you do. As a woman who has accomplished so much and has changed the world around her, she wants to be remembered as someone with integrity who worked hard to find common ground.

"I am passionate about my career and devoted to my family. Balance is something moms know innately. I don't want to give up any of my commitment to my work, and I don't want to give up any time parenting my kids for the brief period they are living with us."

—Justice Bridget McCormack

LYNN POVICH

Lynn Povich is an iconic feminist figure. She has advocated for equal rights for women her whole life. She defied society in the late 60s and early 70s by suing *Newsweek* on the basis that women were not being treated fairly in the work place. She, along with a large group of women who worked at *Newsweek*, took a stand against the advantages men were receiving, but women were not being able to participate in these same advantages. Lynn is an inspiration to all people to this day, especially young women in the workforce. She reminds us that even though most people do not realize it, discrimination against women is still happening. It occurs in less obvious ways and on a subconscious level. She believes that this subtle discrimination can be overcome as long as someone keeps speaking out and standing up for what is fair.

Lynn Povich is motivated to seek fairness in all aspects of life. She believes that kindness is a virtue, and that people should see others for their capabilities, not their gender or race. During the 60s and 70s with the lawsuit at *Newsweek*, her inspiration for going through the whole process was to make the working environment more equal for both men and women. She saw that even though women possessed the same abilities, they were not receiving the same salaries or promotions as their male counterparts. This inequality motivated her to join with other women to file the lawsuit against *Newsweek*.

After the lawsuit, Lynn continued her advocacy for the equal treatment of women in the workplace. She reflects on how she raised her own children. She recalls how there were pros and cons to working part time while raising them. It was good because she was able to spend time with her children, but she also had to pay a price for that decision. While she was working part time, the next generation of workers moved up and received the

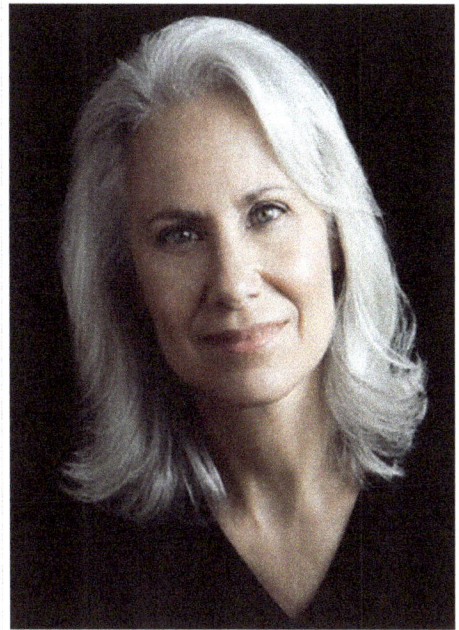

promotions instead of her. Lynn believes that for a woman, life is about compromises. You can have it all, but not at the same time. She advocates for the fair treatment of pregnant women who are on family leave, and she believes that they should have flexibility to continue their job once they return to work. She hopes that this generation of women will accomplish this goal.

Lynn grew up in Washington DC. She said, "Well, when I was 13, I wanted to be a ballerina." Her dance instructor encouraged her to move to New York to attend ballet school. Instead, Lynn decided to stay and continue to be a student. She was a very bright young girl, as were many at the time, but the problem was that it was uncommon for women to actually have a career. It was expected of women to get married, have children, and not continue work. Despite this, Lynn went to Vassar College in the hopes of having a quality education with the other women students enrolled at the school. Her father, Shirley Povich, was an accomplished journalist for the *Washington Post*. Because her father was already a well-known journalist, she wanted to enter a new field. However, by the time she graduated and entered the workforce, she realized she enjoyed writing, and before she knew it, she was a secretary at *Newsweek*. But she did not realize the environment she was about to encounter.

Imagine this: you are one of the few women working for one of the largest and most famous news magazines of your time. The year is 1970, and you work for *Newsweek*. This may be difficult to imagine on its own, but envision also filing a lawsuit against this powerful news media corporation for sex discrimination. This was Lynn Povich's situation along with forty-five other women. But not only did she sue the company, she also continued working for them. She and the forty-five other women won their lawsuit. This, however, was not enough for Lynn. She was concerned that the lawsuit did not accomplish enough to have an impact on her coworkers. So, she sued a second time.

After the lawsuits, she was promoted to senior editor of *Newsweek*, a huge achievement for Lynn Povich and a significant step for women's rights. She

became the first female senior editor of *Newsweek*. While juggling children and a stressful job, she also wrote a book *Good Girls Revolt*. Her inspiring book told the story of the lawsuits and her time working for *Newsweek*. After her role as senior editor, she switched to working as the editor in chief of *The Working Woman*. She also joined MSNBC.com, where she oversaw NBC's digital content. Then she won the Matrix Award for *Magazines*. Now, she is retired at her home in New York.

Lynn Povich wholeheartedly believes that women must stay true to their ideals. Her lawsuit against *Newsweek* demonstrates her commitment to women's rights. Lynn Povich's persistence defines her inner self. She also has worked for several other women's organizations that have advocated equal rights for women.

Lynn Povich is an amazing woman dedicated to making equal opportunities available to everyone. She has worked as the senior editor of *Newsweek*, as the editor in chief of *The Working Women*, and has won several notable awards. Lynn Povich has been on the frontline to advocate for women's rights. She believes that women should be willing to take risks for their principles. She is an extraordinary woman who offers everyone an example of the strength to follow convictions when advocating for basic human rights.

"The struggle was personally painful and professionally scary."

—Lynn Povich

ARLYCE SEIBERT

Smart, responsible, and an inspiration. These are just a few words to describe the amazing leader—Arlyce Seibert. Born and raised in Parma, Ohio, Arlyce Seibert was inspired at a young age to become a teacher and to become involved with education. As a child, she was often found playing school with her friends. Arlyce, who attended an all-girls middle school, talks about the impact her teachers had on her life. She had the opportunity to witness, firsthand, strong women who influenced her life as she became an adult.

Arlyce learned from a very young age that it is important to express your opinions and speak out for what you think is right. In high school, she joined a debate team that was primarily managed by boys. But this did not discourage her in the least. Arlyce quickly excelled and was named an outstanding delegate for her team. "Debate," she says, "allowed me to not personalize my opinions." She believes that it is important to be able to express your ideas and to take risks with them, but not take it personally when someone disagrees with your views. Later, in college, she earned a bachelor of arts degree from the University of Detroit. She also received her master of arts in teaching from Oakland University.

Throughout her life, Arlyce has been influenced and encouraged by men and women who only saw the best in her. Her husband played an important role in her life by providing love and support. In addition to her husband, Arlyce found guidance in Dr. Lillian Bowder, who appointed her as head of Cranbrook's upper school, and later as head of schools at Cranbrook. Arlyce has been in the Cranbrook community for more than forty years.

In 1971 Arlyce began a meteoric career at Cranbrook Schools. She started as a history teacher. Cranbrook had a stellar reputation in education, and Arlyce quickly became impressed with every aspect of this dynamic school. As time went on, Arlyce became the head of the history department at the school. Six years later, she became the director of curriculum. She then became head of the upper school. Finally, she became the head of schools, which is her current position at Cranbrook.

Arlyce Seibert has worked tirelessly and tenaciously to accomplish what she has achieved as a respected education leader in the Cranbrook system. As head of schools at Cranbrook, Arlyce is in charge of all students attending any of the schools on campus. This includes students from age three to the seniors in high school. Arlyce states that the best part of Cranbrook is the people who make up the Cranbrook community. She appreciates that the faculty is amazingly gifted and that Cranbrook fosters strong relationships between students, parents, and teachers. This characteristic is what makes Cranbrook such a wonderful learning environment.

She commented on how she continues to maintain personal relationships with some of her former students and their parents from her earliest years as a teacher at Cranbrook. Arlyce shared her memory of how she received a telephone call from a bus driver at the University of Michigan. He said that he could always identify the students who were former Cranbrook students, because they were gracious and never forgot to say thank you and show their appreciation for those around them.

Arlyce describes Cranbrook in one word—community. Cranbrook is not just a school, but a place in which people genuinely care and support students, and where faculty work together to achieve excellence to harness the creativity and genius of all students. This bond of trust between students, parents, and faculty unites everyone who belongs to the Cranbrook community. Arlyce is proud to state that, "We motivate students from diverse backgrounds to strive for intellectual, creative, and physical excellence, to develop a deep appreciation for the arts and different cultures, and to employ the technological tools of our modern age." She firmly believes that Cranbrook's mission is to encourage students to explore and think for themselves. They will need these tools to become leaders of the future.

In her daily life, Arlyce adheres to three school mottos, "Look to the bees and follow," "Aim high," and "Enter to learn, go forth to serve." She keeps in mind these words as she goes about her day. A typical day for Arlyce includes at least three to four meetings, at which she speaks with other administration and faculty members regarding financial decisions, as well as planning sessions. She is seldom in her office throughout the day. Yet, she is always available to those who want to talk to her, especially students. This commitment to students takes precedence over all other obligations. That is why she continues to be a student advisor to thirteen students each year. Arlyce also continues to create strong emotional bonds with all of the students at Cranbrook. Every year, she attends the graduation of the seniors in the upper school. As the students make their way to the podium to accept their diplo-mas, her heart swells with pride, for she has known many of them for so long. She is proud of every single student, as she recalls the flood of memories she has of them growing up, and maturing into strong, successful adults.

Arlyce Seibert belongs to numerous organizations and has received many awards throughout her career in education. She is presently a member of The Headmasters Association and on the Board of Independent Schools Association of the Central States. She is also the vice president of the Executive Board of the Association of Independent Michigan Schools, as well as president and a regent of the Cum Laude Society. Arlyce has won numerous awards such as the Spirit of Detroit Award and the Dawkins award. Even with all these distinctions, the award that has the most significance is her being named Outstanding Head of School by Columbia University. Arlyce Seibert felt that this was not only an achievement for her, but a recognition for the whole Cranbrook educational community. It was an honor for her to be able to represent Cranbrook, especially since she is one of few female heads of schools. Because there are not many other female heads of schools, Arlyce Seibert feels a great responsibility for her position. Since she became head of schools, the number of female head of schools has increased, and she hopes to see that number increase even more, as more opportunities open up for women around the world.

Another amazing thing about the Cranbrook community is the growth mind-set. Although Arlyce Seibert is already extremely successful in her work with education, she continues to learn from others. She often goes to visit other schools and meets with board members, in the effort to further enhance and improve teaching styles and the way students learn. She applies the new insights to Cranbrook. Arlyce believes that there are many ways to learn and that education is endlessly evolving. In the years to come at Cranbrook, Arlyce is striving to develop plans for an innovation center. She hopes that the center will be a place to better serve performing arts, as well as improve sports.

To all students and youth of this generation who hope to make a difference in the world, she has given simple, yet profound advice. "Go for it.

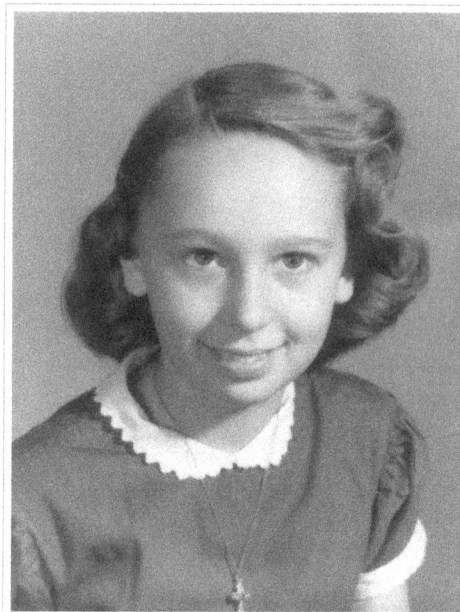

Don't be discouraged." She thinks that it is important to do what you love, and be confident no matter what roadblocks stand in your way.

"Go for it. Don't be discouraged."

—Arlyce Seibert

LOU ANNA K. SIMON

"Listening, learning, and being curious are things that prepare you for almost any kind of job," asserts Lou Anna K. Simon, first woman president of Michigan State University. Listen. Learn. Be curious. President Simon also clutches a moral gyroscope, which is similar to a moral compass. The gyroscope spins, and when the situation changes with the environment, it wobbles, maybe changes course, but it continues to guide. "You have to try things, but, at the same time, you have to know what's right and wrong." This strong conviction and morality has led to President Simon's success in her position as president of Michigan State University.

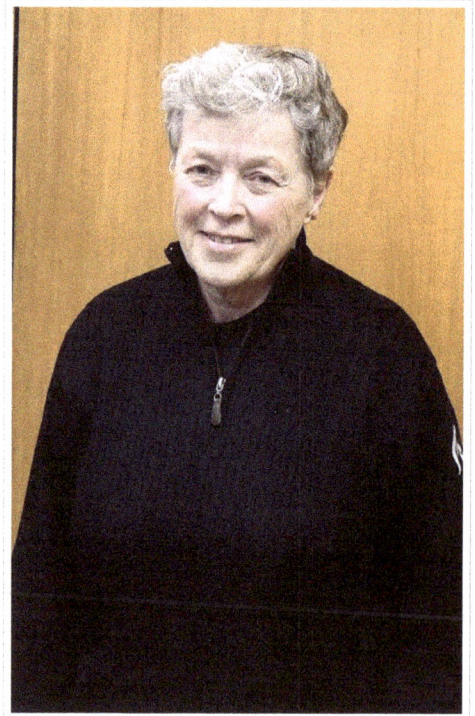

The 1950s and 60s were tough times for women, but President Simon managed to cope with this harsh environment. Growing up in rural Indiana, her family was poor. Her father worked in power plants causing the family to move frequently. Even so, her grandparents and parents stressed that she would go to college, affirming "this is the big dream for you." President Simon would become a first generation college student. Nevertheless, her journey was not easy. Her love of learning began when she spent summers with her grandparents in their small town. There was a Carnegie Library where the librarian let her read anything, with no limits. From those experiences, Dr. Simon was able to develop her skills and confidence that would help her achieve success.

Thankfully, her parents did not stereotype by gender, and they encouraged her to explore her interests regardless of gender. President Simon recalls how she was perceived as different because she played football, used a chemistry set, and helped build a race car. In her early life, these activities were unusual for a girl. She remembers being shunned by classmates over her willingness to explore nontraditional female activities.

She explains how she coped with the iso-
lation: "I just did my thing." She said that
sometimes she needed people to protect her
when she was doing her non-traditional
activities. She needed support and protection
to engage in these activities so she would not
be intimidated by outsiders.

One of the greatest gifts she received from
her parents was the opportunity to explore
new and interesting activities. She zealously
and enthusiastically participated in these
endeavors. President Simon candidly said
that sometimes she felt sad because she was
different. Yet, she would rally because her
teachers, parents, and people around her
gave her the courage and strength to believe
in herself. She also knew that even though
she was teased, she had to be respectful to the bullies. When talking about
her parents, Dr. Simon said, "They were able to turn unusual into special."

President Simon's road through college was nonlinear. She graduated
from a rural high school where the guidance counselor was the football
coach. He helped her decide that she would go to Indiana State since it was
about thirty miles away, which would minimize costs, and that was all her
family could afford. Later, President Simon was given a full scholarship. She
wanted to be a physical education teacher and play basketball. When she
found out that she would also have to take dance classes, she switched to
being a math major. This transition from physical education to math was a
giant leap.

Yet, she selected math because she was one of the few students to have a
rare opportunity to take calculus in her high school. When Dr. Simon
graduated, she did not want to be a teacher. She had minored in science
and chemistry. To her surprise, there were few non-teaching jobs available
for young women in 1969. Thus, in order to obtain a job, President Simon
had to work and obtain a master's degree. The advanced degree enabled her
to be a school counselor.

It is a wonder to Dr. Simon how her life's journey led her to MSU. Her
introduction to the university was a unique experience. The vice president of
Indiana State had a connection with a person at MSU and told him about
President Simon and that she had a math degree. President Simon went to
MSU and interviewed with a gentleman, and he then sent her to lunch with
a few women. Two weeks later, Dr. Simon was offered a job, and in her
words she "has had odd jobs ever since" with titles such as provost and now
president! President Simon's childhood and educational path teach us that

no matter how we are brought up, we can build a fabulous series of accomplishments.

Throughout her ten-year term, President Simon has changed MSU in many ways. Driven by her will to make the world a better place for the next generation, MSU has expanded its research in many subjects including green energy, medical technology, safe water, and agriculture (to decrease world hunger). Dr. Simon has ensured that MSU makes a significant positive impact worldwide. When asked about her own goals for the university, her immediate response was that she wants to make it better tomorrow than it is today, and to do it with the values that we all think are important, to always expect a higher level of quality, to be very inclusive in our thoughts and the way we do things. President Simon shared her insight about her leadership style, "You never have to agree, you can listen, but you don't have to agree." With this leadership approach, her steadfastness in following her moral gyroscope, and her natural curiosity, President Simon is truly an amazing woman and a great leader for Michigan State University, and for the world.

President Simon believes that a strong leader is a person who is genuine and truthful to oneself and to others. A true leader must always have others' interests at heart. They also must put others' needs ahead of their own. In doing so, the leader develops followers. Her advice to women in leadership roles is to have a moral gyroscope, be kind, and put others before you. In President Simon's words, "Do not do things only for you, but also for others."

President Lou Anna K. Simon is curious and determined. She keeps her successes low key and embraces many different kinds of experiences. But her essence is her unique sense of inquisitiveness and adventure. Listening. Learning. Curiosity. We learned that these three things, along with a steady and well-oriented moral gyroscope are key factors to success. They were essential on her path from working on data collection, to her research positions, to being provost, and finally, to becoming president of Michigan State University. The same traits are guiding her as she continues to improve the university. Her lessons remind us to nurture the opportunities, to listen, learn and be curious, weld together our own moral gyroscope, give it a good spin, find success, and make the world a better place in which to live.

"Listening, learning, and being curious are things that prepare you for almost any kind of job."

—MSU President Lou Anna K. Simon

KYM WORTHY

Kym Worthy is a remarkable woman. She is the second African American to serve as the Wayne County prosecutor in Michigan, and the first woman to hold this position. Kym Worthy possesses tremendous leadership qualities and the ability to face challenges—the two major attributes that one needs in order to be successful. Kym Worthy inspires us to be courageous in the pursuit of a career. She embraces these qualities through her actions in many tough and controversial cases that she has prosecuted.

For example, she charged and successfully prosecuted ex-mayor of Detroit, Kwame M. Kilpatrick, and his former chief of staff, Christine Beatty. The case garnered national and international press coverage. She was brave in her commitment to prosecute this case. She received several threats on her life throughout the course of this case, but has been widely acknowledged for her courage and integrity in the litigation of this case that could have negatively impacted her political career. Kym Worthy was named one of "America's Best and Brightest" by two nationally-circulated magazines, and has received over one hundred other awards and honors for her public service and community leadership. Kym Worthy conceived and implemented a "Change the Culture," initiative that focuses on educational training and community policing in an effort to reduce gun violence in the Detroit community. Recognizing that "service is the rent we pay for living," Kym Worthy created the Alexandra Simone Fund for the Neonatal Intensive Care Unit of Henry Ford Hospital in memory of her deceased daughter.

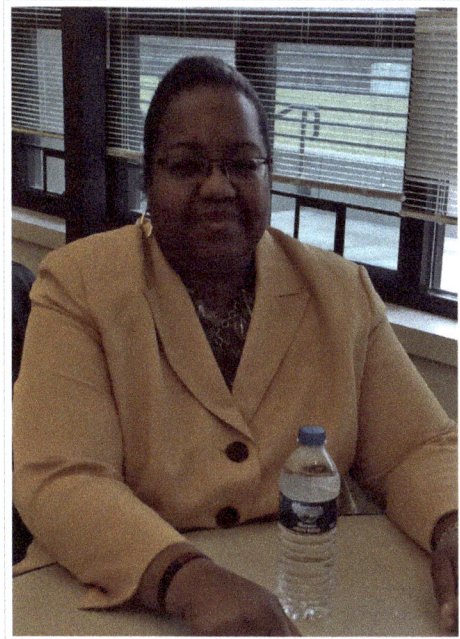

Most people wonder from where Kym Worthy draws her inspiration in living her life. She responds, "True equality is having diversity in every area of the courtroom." Her passion for law began in middle school. She had no plans of becoming a criminal prosecutor. However, she found herself drawn to this area of practice. Many people have also inspired her to pursue a career in the law. Every year, while she was in law school, the African American students had an Alumni Weekend. Prosecutors in the 1970s did not have racial or sex diversity in the prosecutorial office. Her observation that there were very few African Americans and even fewer women who worked in the courtroom caused Kym Worthy to become an advocate to open doors to these individuals.

Kym Worthy talked about her childhood and education. In her early life her father was in the military and had a high rank. Therefore, he and his African American family gained much respect. Kym Worthy stated, "Racism still exists ... I hope that now people accept others for what and who they are." Kym Worthy's career started when she went to law school at Notre Dame, where inequality played a big role in her experiences there. When asked about them, she replied that "there weren't many African Americans or colored people going to law school in the 1970s; in fact, it was very unusual for people of color to be present." Kym Worthy talks about her frustration with the fact that women and people of color were not very common on the college campus. Moreover, she describes her drive for equality, in terms of gender and race. She believes that judgment based on gender still exists in today's society. To support this statement, she explained how in several businesses, and other work environments, some women still do not receive the same pay as men who are performing the same work, and "these are the struggles of being a woman."

Kym Worthy has dedicated her life work to being a very successful prosecuting attorney of Wayne County. She has had a very powerful impact on this community. For example, she has been a role model for women interested in pursuing a career in law. She has also been an advocate for rape victims. She has tried many rape cases. Recently she found a stash of rape kits that are thirty years old, which have not been laboratory tested to determine the likely criminal through DNA testing. Few women report rape, so it is very difficult to get many of the rapists convicted. But funds have come that will help test three thousand rape kits that have never been analyzed. This will have a significant impact on prosecuting rape cases, because the DNA evidence can be examined to identify the person who committed the crime.

Kym Worthy made the decision to become a prosecuting attorney. This career choice sparked her passion as she pursued her life's calling. She says, "Good things can only come if you open your mind and let them in." She reminds us that we should expand our horizon and keep an eye out for other interests. For example, Kym Worthy wanted to be a lawyer for a long time. She said that she thought that English would be an important class. Yet, she also considered history. Kym Worthy explains that we need to understand the history of our government to advance legal positions. She states, "Just when you think you've figured something out, think about it again and again because people change their mind all the time. It's just that some are afraid to take another route."

She believes that having excellent speaking skills are important. The ability to speak to people is essential to communicating your ideas to others. She also emphasized that using proper grammar and having superior writing ability are key skills to being a great lawyer. Most importantly, however, a person should be able to embrace every new opportunity, even small ones, to advance his or her career.

Kym Worthy is successful, talented, and a thoughtful person. When asked, "What recent phenomenon contributes to the problems you deal with in court?" she answered, "The evolution of technology." She believes that in today's society, where technology is constantly advancing, that children are developing poor problem solving skills, along with bad ideas. She also stated, "The most important thing is for a child to respect themselves; only then will others respect them." This means a child should take affirmative steps to always improve themselves. Kym Worthy stated that respect comes when it is returned to others. In addition, when people constantly improve and grow into better people, it becomes easier to respect yourself. Kym Worthy also believes that if you respect yourself, you will gain more confidence. She says that better people will help society in new and creative ways. Kym Worthy is truly a remarkable, talented, hardworking, and successful woman who has inspired everyone, proving that women can make a change in the world.

"Racism still exists . . . I hope that now people accept others for what and who they are."

—Wayne County Chief Prosecutor Kym Worthy

DR. XIANGQUN ZENG

Dr. Xiangqun Zeng is a renowned analytical chemist and electrochemist living in Michigan. Her first name, Xiangqun, means "learning from people." This name prophesied her lifelong ambition to learn from others in order to contribute to the rich body of analytical chemistry and electrochemistry research. It was a difficult journey especially since she grew up in a traditional Chinese culture, in which few women forged a career in science.

When asked, "What is the source of your inspiration," Dr. Zeng's immediate response was, "My mother. She gave me the dream." Frequently, people in her parents' generation were unable to attend a university because universities were closed during the Cultural Revolution. The Chinese government began a program to relocate many young girls and boys to the countryside, which prevented most of
them from participating in careers that required a university education. Dr. Zeng, however, confided that her parents always put education as the highest priority in her family no matter what the circumstances were in China.

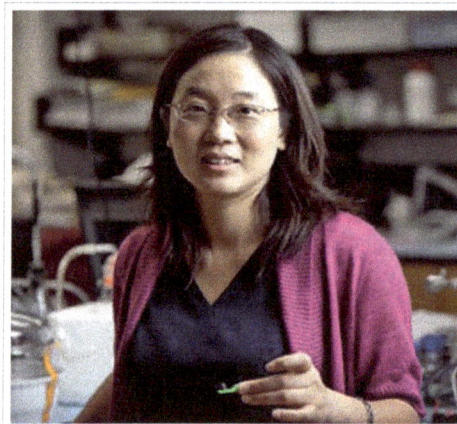

When Dr. Zeng was in elementary school, China experienced tremendous changes. The government opened universities again in 1976 after a decade-long Cultural Revolution that had restricted higher education. Dr. Zeng was a high achiever and was the first in her class all through her middle and high school years. She then attended Chengdu University of Science and Technology in 1985 and majored in Chemistry. She remembered hearing as a young girl in China, "If you study hard and do well in math, physics, and chemistry, you will have a job anywhere, anytime."

In 1989, the year she graduated from college, the "Tiananmen Square Protests" caused the government to block students from going overseas to pursue higher educations. Even this obstacle did not diminish her hope of pursuing her dream. Dr. Zeng went on to obtain her master's degree in chemistry from Beijing Normal University and then obtained a competitive faculty position teaching chemistry at Beijing University of Chemical Technology. In 1994 China's restrictive policy changed, and Dr. Zeng obtained a full scholarship to study chemistry in the United States. This more than fulfilled her dream and was a major, pivotal moment for her scientific achievement and later success. She recalls, "Coming to America was my turning point in achieving my goals." She received her doctorate from State University of New York at Buffalo in only three years and became a full-time professor in 2011 through an early promotion at Oakland University in Michigan.

The freedom of thought encouraged in science has allowed Dr. Zeng to fully develop her research acumen and skills, which has opened many doors for her. Science allows her to interact with people all over the world in various disciplines. The attack on the United States on September 11, 2001, was a triggering catalyst for Dr. Zeng's research in sensors due to the increasing needs of new sensor technology. Sensors offer an almost unlimited ability to provide immediate feedback about the world around us. They are critical for a broad range of applications, including national security, health care, the environment, energy, food safety, and manufacturing. She focused her research on developing low cost, reliable sensors to detect death-killing chemicals by integrating innovative sensing materials with miniaturized analysis platforms that combine high performance, miniaturized electrodes and instrumentation electronics with multi-transduction-mode sensor array devices. She is open to new ideas and innovations and explores different scientific viewpoints working with a multidisciplinary team of scientists and engineers. This and her drive for success has made her a leader in her field.

One of Dr. Zeng's discoveries includes the novel molecular design of a range of materials to manufacture new sensing surfaces. These state-of-the-art sensing surfaces offer the far-reaching capability to detect a broad range of components in a gas, liquid, or solid, such as methane, bacteria, and cancer biomarkers. For example, Dr. Zeng's biosensor work allows the monitoring of chemicals in the human blood samples at the point of care. Once fully developed, this sensor would be able to detect if a person has cancer. If treatment for cancer has begun, the sensor would monitor the chemotherapy and regulate the appropriate drug levels during treatment of the patient.

Dr. Zeng is eager to have a variety of sensors available for commercial use within five years. She explains, "I am working on sensors ranging from detecting bacterial pathogens for infectious disease diagnostics to methane for energy and work safety monitoring." She is also experimenting with ways of using various sensor materials to make a sensor as sensitive and selective as a human nose. One example of this is that she is creating an electronic sensor that is able to detect methane and other chemicals.

Methane, the main component of natural gas, is the major cause for coal mine explosions and is also a green-house gas. This is why this device would be so important to energy, safety, and climate change. A highly sensitive sensor would be able to detect small levels of methane emission and save lives and the environment.

Dr. Zeng's competitive nature comes from her early participation in competitive sports. She encourages sports as a character building experience stating that, "Sports trained me to be both physically and mentally strong. We had practice competition every day which taught me to not be afraid of failures and learn from them. When I experience rejection, which in grant writing is often for a scientist, I don't get down and I never give up. Sports also build team skills which are very important. You need good interpersonal skills, a positive attitude and high energy levels to accomplish your goals."

As a woman who has traveled so far to accomplish so much, Dr. Zeng offers these words to people of all ages, "You need to learn as much as possible. Science needs women in leadership roles. To succeed in science, you need to have technical skills and be confident; otherwise, men won't listen to you." Not only is Dr. Zeng making new and exciting inroads within her research, she is also strongly involved in scientific community service and outreach and educating others about science.

She has mentored students and research scholars from all over the world at various levels and backgrounds, training them with the knowledge and skill set needed for the next-generation workforce. Her tireless pursuit of excellence reflects in her students and program growth and successes. Her remarkable aptitude to think beyond basic science and toward solving pervasive challenges in modern society has impressed her peers and those she has supervised.

She has received many awards for her work, including the Oakland University Young Investigator Research Excellence Award in 2005, Academic Excellence Recognition Awards in 2011 and 2012, Research Excellence Award in 2015, and International Service Award in 2015. Dr. Zeng ranks among the few women who have selected a nontraditional career path in the field of chemistry. Her great energy and enthusiasm as well as her commitment to excellence allow her to become a pioneer in the advancement of new analytical technology to improve clinical and

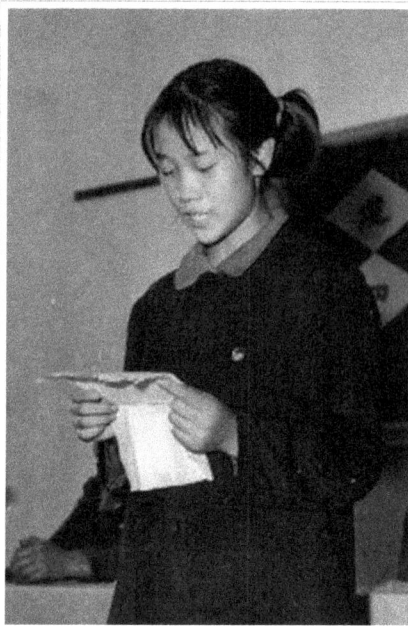

environmental monitoring. She is on the cutting edge of science and always pushing for a deeper understanding of science, sensors, and social issues.

"You need to learn as much as possible. Science needs women in leadership roles. To succeed in science you need to have technical skills and be confident .... "

—Dr. Xiangqun Zeng

STUDENT AUTHORS

Sofia Adams
Mahshad Afshar
Skylar K. Allison
Yasmeen Amjad
Srujana Annavarapu
Kalah Brown
Rhea Dhar
Bree Gross
Sofie Harb
Zehra Husaini
Swathi Karthik
Isabel Mantese
Simrin Nagaraju
Claire Pearce
Helen Qin
Elizabeth Reese
Lena Roberts
Surina Sheth
Paige Tar
Eleanor Townsend
Mary Townsend
Natalie Wilcox
Dina Zreik

ADULT AUTHOR-DIRECTORS

Gerard Mantese
Theresamarie Mantese
Gregory Nowakowski

www.ingramcontent.com/pod-product-compliance
Lightning Source LLC
Chambersburg PA
CBHW060945100426

42813CB00016B/2872